¡Viva el español!

Workbook

¡Hola!

John De Mado
Linda Tibensky

Jane Jacobsen-Brown
Christine Wolinski Szeszol
Donna Alfredo Wardanian

Marcela Gerber, Series Consultant

 **Wright Group**

The McGraw·Hill Companies

www.WrightGroup.com

Mc Graw Hill Wright Group

Copyright ©2005 Wright Group/McGraw-Hill

Printed in the United States of America.

Send all inquiries to:
Wright Group/McGraw-Hill
P.O. Box 812960
Chicago, Illinois 60681

ISBN: 0-07-600286-1

2 3 4 5 6 7 8 9 POH 10 09 08 07 06 05 04

Contenido

Unidad 4

Unidad 5

Unidad 6

Repaso Unidades 4–6

Unidad 7

¿Cómo se dice?

Nombre _____

A. You heard a conversation about Arturo, Rosa, and señorita Jiménez. Unscramble the letters below the answer blank to form a word and complete each statement you heard.

M ¿Cómo se llama la _____chica_____?
acihc

1. Se _____malla_____ Rosa.

2. ¿_____omóC_____ se llama la señorita?

3. Se llama _____ñosetari_____ Jiménez.

4. El _____icohc_____ se llama Arturo.

B. You are the teacher and there are five new students in class. Find out what their names are. Write the answers on the lines below.

M **a.** ¿Cómo te llamas?
   b. Me llamo Carlos.

El niño se llama Carlos. _____

1. _____

2. _____

3. _____

4. _____

5. _____

¿Cómo se dice?

Nombre _____

A. It's very noisy around school today. You can only hear one half of each conversation. What do you think the other person is saying? Choose the question or answer that should complete the conversation. Write its letter in the empty balloon.

a. ¿Cómo estás?
b. ¡Buenos días!
c. Me llamo Beto.
d. ¿Cómo te llamas?

e. ¿Cómo se llama el chico?
f. Muy bien, gracias.
g. ¡Buenas tardes!
h. ¡Hola!

M 1.

2.

3.

4.

5.

¿Cómo se dice?

Nombre _____

B. Andrés and María are trying to hold a conversation. Help them out by finding the word that is missing. Write the word on the line.

pronto	gracias	llamo	Buenas
Cómo	luego	✓ Hola	días

Ⓜ ANDRÉS: _____ **¡Hola!** _____ ¿Cómo estás?

1. MARÍA: Buenos _____.

2. Bien, _____.

3. ANDRÉS: ¿_____ te llamas?

4. MARÍA: Me _____ María.

5. ANDRÉS: Hasta _____, María.

6. MARTA: Hasta _____, Andrés.

C. Someone has erased the punctuation marks on your page! Choose the punctuation marks that go with each line. Then write the marks on the line.

Ⓜ LUIS: **¡Buenas tardes!**

1. **Cómo te llamas**

2. ELENA: **Buenas tardes**

3. **Me llamo Elena**

4. **Y tú, cómo te llamas**

5. LUIS: **Me llamo Luis**

6. ELENA: **Adiós, Luis**

7. LUIS: **Hasta pronto**

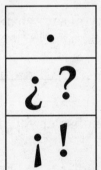

¿Cómo se dice?

Nombre _____

D. You and your friends greet each other every day. To keep from getting bored, try to change greetings. Write at least one or two responses to each statement.

M ¡Adiós! _____ **¡Hasta luego! ¡Hasta pronto!** _____

1. ¡Hola! _____

2. ¿Cómo estás? _____

3. ¡Hasta mañana! _____

4. ¿Qué tal? _____

¡Piénsalo!

1. Circle the greeting you would use at 7:30 in the morning.

     Buenas tardes.   Buenos días.   Buenas noches.

2. What do you say when someone asks you this question: **¿Cómo te llamas?**

    _____

3. Circle the answer you might give if someone asks you this question: **¿Cómo estás?**

     ¡Hasta luego!   Se llama Juan.   Muy bien, gracias.

4. Circle the greeting you would use at 9:00 at night.

     Buenas tardes.   Buenos días.   Buenas noches.

¿Cómo se dice?

Nombre _____

A. Rosalía and Rodrigo are making a picture of their classroom. To check what they have included, write the number next to the correct word in the lists below. One has already been done for you.

M __2__ la luz

____ el pizarrón

____ la computadora

____ el pupitre

____ el escritorio

____ la puerta

____ la silla

¿Cómo se dice?   Nombre _____

B. Draw your own classroom! Label each object or person next to its picture.

¿Cómo se dice?

Nombre _____

A. Help Josefina finish the labels for her pictures. Read the sentence and write in the missing letters to complete the label.

M Es el es <u>c</u> <u>r</u> <u>i</u> torio.

1. Es el ___ ___ ___ arrón.

2. Es el m___ ___ ___ tro.

Es un ___ ___ ___ bre.

3. Es el a___ ___ ___ no.

4. Es la ___ ___ ll ___.

5. Es la ma___ ___ ___ ra.

Es una mu___ ___ ___.

¿Cómo se dice?

Nombre _____

B. Paco wants to ask you about the classroom, but he doesn't always ask the right question. Help him out. Circle the letter of the question he should ask.

M   Es la computadora.
    ⓐ ¿Qué es?
    b. ¿Quién es?

1. Es la luz.
    a. ¿Qué es?
    b. ¿Quién es?

2. Es la alumna.
    a. ¿Qué es?
    b. ¿Quién es?

3. Es el maestro.
    a. ¿Qué es?
    b. ¿Quién es?

4. Es el escritorio.
    a. ¿Qué es?
    b. ¿Quién es?

5. Es la silla.
    a. ¿Qué es?
    b. ¿Quién es?

6. Es la maestra.
    a. ¿Qué es?
    b. ¿Quién es?

C. Hortensia fell asleep in class and doesn't know all the words! How do you answer her questions? Write the answer to the question on the lines. If the answer is no, write the correct one.

M   ¿Es el pupitre?

No, no es el pupitre. Es el alumno.

M   ¿Es el escritorio?

Sí, es el escritorio.

1. ¿Es la alumna?

_____

2. ¿Es la luz?

_____

3. ¿Es la silla?

_____

4. ¿Es el libro?

_____

¿Cómo se dice?

Nombre _____

A. This classroom is really crowded! Count the items you see and write the words for the numbers you have counted.

M _____tres_____ pizarrones

_____ alumnos y alumnas   _____ computadoras

_____ niños   _____ puertas

_____ niñas   _____ sillas

_____ maestros   _____ luces

_____ escritorio   _____ pupitres

¡Piénsalo!

Circle the highest number in each row.

1. catorce   quince   trece   veinte

2. nueve   diez   siete   cuatro

3. dieciséis   dieciocho   diecisiete   once

4. dos   veintidós   doce   veintitrés

¿Cómo se dice?

Nombre _____

A. Pepito's computer is broken. It has changed all the numerals of his addition problems into words. Change the words into numbers.

M Cuatro más uno es cinco.

$4 + 1 = 5$

1. Diez más dos es doce.

_____

2. Once más diez es veintiuno.

_____

Now Pepito needs words, and the computer will only write numbers! Write the addition problems with words.

M $7 + 8 = 15$

Siete más ocho es quince.

1. $9 + 14 = 23$

2. $1 + 12 = 13$

B. Luisa has called to ask you for the telephone numbers of some classmates. Before you read them to her, write down the words for each number.

M Víctor: 342-8732

tres, cuatro, dos, ocho, siete, tres, dos

1. Juanita: 863-5060

_____

2. Anselmo: 585-9864

_____

3. Timoteo: 765-8743

_____

¿Qué es?

Nombre _____

No es un hombre ni una mujer, no es una niña ni un niño, ¿qué es?

"¡Hola, amigos! Todo el día escucho: hola, adiós, buenos días, buenas tardes, buenas noches, hasta pronto, hasta luego y hasta mañana. Estoy en el escritorio. ¡Estoy muy bien! Mi número es el cuatro, cinco, tres, dos, siete, cero, cuatro. Me llaman y sueno RIIIIIIIINNNN . . ."

1. ¿Es una niña?

_____

2. ¿Es un pizarrón?

_____

3. ¿Cuál es su número?

_____

4. ¿Cómo está?

_____

5. ¿Qué es?

_____

**Draw the answer
to the riddle
in the box.**

¡A DIVERTIRSE! Nombre _____

Busca el número

Find the name of the number in each row. Draw a circle around the word that names the number on the left. Follow the model by tracing the circle.

7   tres   ocho   dos   (siete)   cuatro

5   cinco   tres   quince   seis   uno

12   ocho   dos   once   doce   siete

4   veinte   cuatro   diez   catorce   dos

13   nueve   tres   trece   cinco   uno

Conexión con las matemáticas

Write the number that is missing to make each problem correct. You can write out the sums in numbers as a hint!

M Cinco más _____cuatro_____ es nueve.

1. Diez más _____ es quince.

2. Once más _____ es veinte.

3. _____ más doce es veintiséis.

4. _____ más cuatro es veintiuno.

5. Veintitrés más _____ es veintinueve.

¿Cómo se dice?   Nombre _____

A. Claudia made a poster of her classroom. Now she's teaching her mother about the things there are in her classroom. Read each sentence, and then draw a line from the sentence to the correct picture.

El salón de clase

M **1.** Es la bandera.

2. Es el borrador.

3. Es la papelera.

4. Es el globo.

5. Es el mapa.

6. Es el marcador.

7. Es la mesa.

8. Es la pared.

¡Piénsalo!

Circle the largest object in each row. Draw a box around the smallest object in each row.

1. el borrador   la ventana   el reloj

2. el pupitre   el globo   la tiza

3. la tiza   el mapa   la puerta

4. la mesa   la papelera   la pared

¿Cómo se dice?   Nombre _____

A. Mario has a messy desk! How in the world can he fit so many things in his
desk? Tell Mario what he has. On the line beside each number, write the name
of the object with that number. The first one is done for you.

1. Tienes un libro. _____

2. _____

3. _____

4. _____

5. _____

6. _____

7. _____

¿Cómo se dice?   Nombre _____

A. Sergio is preparing a report about his classroom. Help him complete his sentences. Choose the word you would use to complete the sentence according to the picture. Write the word in the blank.

M En el salón de clase hay una _____bandera_____ .

1. Hay tres _____ .

2. En la pared hay un _____ y dos _____ .

3. En el salón de clase hay un _____ y diez _____ .

ventanas   reloj   maestro   mapas   alumnos   ✓bandera

B. Change the words from Exercise A from one to more than one, or from more than one to one.

M tres ventanas

    una _____ventana_____

1. un reloj

    tres _____

2. dos mapas

    un _____

3. un maestro

    cinco _____

4. diez alumnos

    un _____

Nombre _____

C. Julia needs your help. She doesn't know how to change the words in her list to show more than one. Circle the ending you would add to each word and write the word in the blank.

M mujer   s   (es)   _____mujeres_____

1. hombre   s   es   _____

2. reloj   s   es   _____

3. pared   s   es   _____

4. pupitre   s   es   _____

5. regla   s   es   _____

6. papel   s   es   _____

D. How well can you talk about more than one thing? Decide whether you would use *s* or *es* to talk about more than one to a friend. Write the word in the blank.

M Tienes un televisor.

Tienes dos _____televisores_____.

1. Tienes un marcador.

Tienes dos _____.

2. Tienes un globo.

Tienes dos _____.

3. Tienes un sol.

Tienes dos _____.

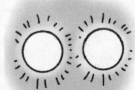

Nombre _____

E. How well do you know your own classroom? Count the number of objects or people. Then write the answer.

M ¿Cuántos mapas hay en el salón de clase?

Hay dos mapas.
_____

1. ¿Cuántas mesas hay en el salón de clase?

_____

2. ¿Cuántas alumnas hay en el salón de clase?

_____

3. ¿Cuántos borradores hay en el pizarrón?

_____

4. ¿Cuántos pupitres hay en el salón de clase?

_____

5. ¿Cuántos relojes hay en las paredes?

_____

F. Now you can write a report about your classroom. Use all the words you have learned. Look at what you wrote in Exercise E, and add some new ideas.

_____

_____

_____

_____

¿Cómo se dice?

Nombre _____

A. It's Visitors' Night at school and you have been assigned the task of making labels for items in the classroom. Write the word *el, los, la,* or *las* on each label.

M

_____**el**_____ cuaderno

1.

_____ ventanas

2.

_____ marcador

3.

_____ escritorios

4.

_____ papeleras

5.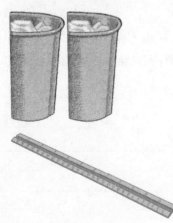

_____ regla

Nombre _____

B. You and your friends are playing "Find the Question." For each answer, find the right question from the box. Then write it on the line above the answer.

M _____¿Quién es?_____

Es el maestro.

¿Qué es?	
¿Qué son?	
¿Quién es?	
¿Quiénes son?	

1. _____

Es un amigo.

2. _____

Son los lápices.

3. _____

Es el salón de clase.

4. _____

Son los pupitres.

5. _____

Son Rogelio y Susana.

6. _____

Es un libro.

7. _____

Son las alumnas.

8. _____

Es una silla.

¡A leer!

Nombre _____

Read the dialogue and answer the questions.

¿Cuántas Marías hay?

MAESTRA: A ver, ¿cuántas niñas hay en el salón de clase? ¿Cómo te llamas tú?

MARÍA A.: ¡Yo me llamo María Amparo!

MARÍA B.: ¡Yo soy María Blanca!

MARÍA C.: ¡Yo me llamo María del Carmen!

MARÍA D.: Y yo soy María Dolores. . .

JOSÉ MARÍA: Yo me llamo José María. . .

NIÑAS: ¡Tú eres un niño!

MAESTRA: ¿Cuántas niñas hay, Mónica?

MÓNICA: Yo, y cuatro Marías.

1. ¿Cuántas niñas hay en el salón de clase?

_____

2. ¿Cuántos alumnos hay en el salón de clase? ¿Cómo se llama el niño?

_____

3. ¿Cuántas maestras hay en el salón de clase?

_____

4. ¿Cuántas Marías hay en el salón de clase?

_____

Now imagine the classroom. On a piece of paper, draw the girls on one side and the boys on the other side. Label each drawing.

Nombre _____

Conexión con las matemáticas

Use the rulers to measure each object. Decide whether the measurement is in centimeters *(centímetros)* or in meters *(metros)*. Use the word *mide* to tell how long each object is.

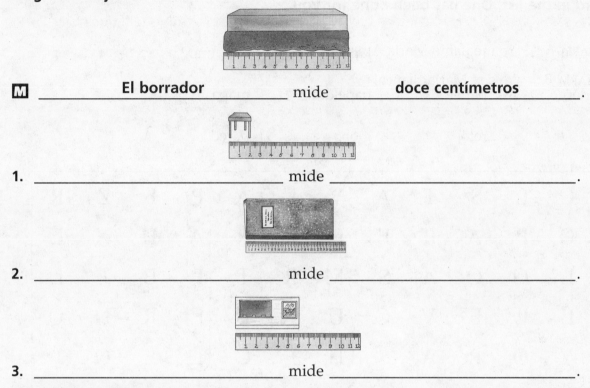

M _____ El borrador _____ mide _____ doce centímetros _____.

1. _____ mide _____.

2. _____ mide _____.

3. _____ mide _____.

⚬ ¡APRENDE MÁS! ⚬

The Spanish alphabet is almost like the one you know in English. But the sounds that the letters stand for are not all the same. In most cases, letters are written the same way. One of the letters stands for a special sound. This letter is different from the ones you know. Look at the alphabet below and circle the letter that is different.

El alfabeto en español

A, a	E, e	I, I	M, m	P, p	T, t	X, x
B, b	F, f	J, j	N, n	Q, q	U, u	Y, y
C, c	G, g	K, k	Ñ, ñ	R, r	V, v	Z, z
D, d	H, h	L, l	O, o	S, s	W, w	

¡A DIVERTIRSE!

Nombre _____

Busca las palabras

Read the words on the list and try to find them in the box. The words are either down or across. When you find a word, circle it and then make a check by the word in the list. One has been done for you.

bolígrafo	regla	lápiz	bandera
cuaderno	✓ papel	papelera	mapa
libro	reloj	globo	pared

```
C L S T A V L Á P I Z R
O P A P E L E R A H X E
L G O A S M R T P B J L
L L E V C U A D E R N O
Y O P A S H E C L E O J
U B Y V W Y B D S G G H
B O L Í G R A F O L L K
N R I N F D N I M A Z Q
T S B G W Y D Z Q R K L
S E R P A R E D E R L O
U I O K Q A R I F Z X I
Z O I M A P A K W Q C U
```

¿Cómo se dice?

Nombre _____

A. Rita drew a picture for her math class, but now she needs to count how many geometric shapes she drew to make Maqui, the robot. Answer the questions.

1. ¿Cuántos cuadrados hay? _____

2. ¿Cuántos círculos hay? _____

3. ¿Cuántos rectángulos hay? _____

4. ¿Cuántos triángulos hay? _____

¿Cómo se dice?

Nombre _____

A. You have entered a contest. If you unscramble the letters and write all the words correctly, you win. Start now!

El flamenco es **_____rosado_____**.

odsaro

1.

El ratón es _____.

isgr

2.

El canario es _____.

riamallo

3.

El oso es _____.

ogner

4.

El loro es _____.

devre

¿Cómo se dice?   Nombre _____

A. Pepito is showing you his coloring book. What can you say about the picture? Color in the picture, then answer the questions.

Ⓜ ¿Cómo es Antonio?

Antonio es grande. _____

1. ¿De qué color es el tigre?

_____

2. ¿De qué color es Pepe?

_____

3. ¿Qué animal es Raúl?

_____

4. ¿Qué animal es el maestro?

_____

5. ¿De qué color es Marcos?

_____

6. ¿Cómo es Raúl?

_____

7. ¿Cómo es Pepe?

_____

8. ¿Cómo es el señor Flamenco?

_____

¿Cómo se dice?

Nombre _____

A. Juanito has written some sentences about his classroom, but he isn't sure about how to write the descriptive words. Help him out. Use the descriptive word in parentheses to complete the sentence. Be sure to write the appropriate form of the word!

M Las reglas son _____ **largas** _____. (largo)

1. El escritorio es _____. (pequeño)

2. La puerta es _____. (blanco)

3. Los bolígrafos son _____. (negro)

4. Las sillas son _____. (azul)

5. La ventana es _____. (grande)

6. Los pizarrones son _____. (verde)

7. Las cestas son _____. (amarillo)

8. Los cuadernos son _____. (anaranjado)

¡Piénsalo! ⌒⌒⌒⌒⌒⌒⌒⌒⌒⌒⌒⌒⌒⌒⌒⌒⌒⌒⌒

Circle the word in each row that does not belong.

1. perro	tigre	oso	pez	azul
2. loro	amarillo	rojo	gris	rosado
3. triángulo	cuadrado	pequeño	rectángulo	círculo
4. largo	corto	grande	ratón	pequeño

Nombre _____

B. There are colors all around you. How many can you name? Complete the sentence by writing the color or colors of the classroom object.

M El lápiz es _____ negro y amarillo _____.

1. El pizarrón es _____.

2. Los pupitres son _____.

3. El cuaderno es _____.

4. La tiza es _____.

C. You're on your own! Make up your own sentences about items in your classroom. You may use colors or other words to describe them.

1. _____

2. _____

3. _____

4. _____

5. _____

¿Cómo se dice?

Nombre _____

A. While you were helping señor Millones clean the attic, you found some treasures. What is in the attic? After looking at each picture, complete the sentence by writing *un, unos, una,* or *unas* in the blank.

M

Hay _____una_____ bandera.

1.

Hay _____ oso.

2.

Hay _____ ratones.

3.

Hay _____ computadoras.

4.

Hay _____ globos.

5.

Hay _____ círculos.

6.

Hay _____ papelera.

Nombre _____

B. These two classrooms are different. Look at A and the sentences below. Color the picture as indicated. Then look at B, color it as you like, and write sentences to describe it.

A

M Hay una ventana grande.

1. Hay un loro verde y azul.

2. Hay unos ratones pequeños.

3. Hay unas computadoras blancas.

4. Hay un círculo negro.

5. Hay una mariposa negra y azul.

6. Hay un globo grande y unas reglas cortas.

B

M _____ Hay unas ventanas grandes. _____

1. _____

2. _____

3. _____

4. _____

Nombre _____

C. The animals from señora Luna's science class have escaped. Where are they now? For each picture, write a question and an answer. (Note: *P* means *Pregunta* or "Question" and *R* means *Respuesta* or "Answer.")

M

P: _____ ¿Qué hay en el pupitre? _____

R: _____ Hay unos loros en el pupitre. _____

1.

P: _____

R: _____

2.

P: _____

R: _____

3.

P: _____

R: _____

4.

P: _____

R: _____

¡A leer!

Nombre _____

Read Sandra's paragraph and list your answers on the chart.

Mi animal favorito

Me llamo Sandra. ¿Cuál es mi animal favorito? Mi animal favorito es el conejo. Los conejos son pequeños y tienen las orejas largas. Hay conejos blancos, negros y marrones. Hay conejos de dos colores. En el salón de clase hay dos conejos. Están en una mesa. ¡Los conejos tienen cuatro conejitos! Los conejitos son conejos muy pequeños. Son bebés.

Nota: **Bebés** means "babies."

¿Cómo son los conejos?	Colores de los conejos

Dibuja los conejos y conejitos en la mesa del salón de clase.

Nombre _____

Conexión con el arte

Color each of these circles with a primary color and see what colors appear where the circles overlap. Write the name of each color in Spanish on the lines. What color do you see in the center?

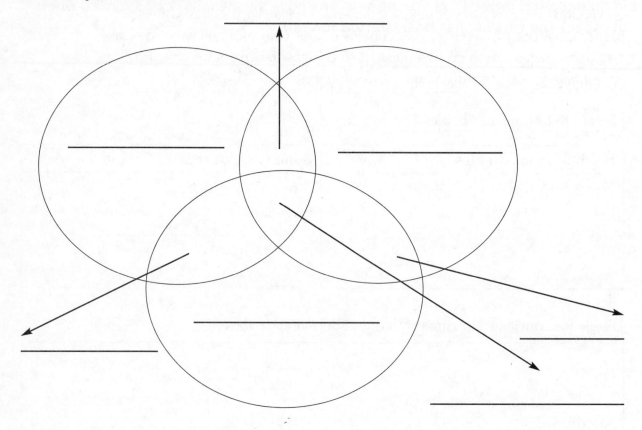

Look at the circles you colored and fill in the blanks with the missing colors:

_____ + amarillo = naranja

_____ + azul = verde

azul + rojo = _____

rojo + amarillo + azul = _____

⸙ ¡APRENDE MÁS! ⸙

Nombre _____

Once you know the alphabet in Spanish, you know how to put words in alphabetical order. And once you know alphabetical order, you will know how to look up words in a dictionary or glossary.

Let's practice. Each list of words is all mixed up. Next to the list, write the words in alphabetical order. (You do not need to know the meaning of a word to put it in order.) The first list has been started for you.

El alfabeto: a, b, c, d, e, f, g, h, i, j, k, 1, m, n, ñ, o, p, q, r, s, t, u, v, w, x, y, z

1. silla _____**alumno**_____   **3.** día _____

libro _____   mañana _____

alumno _____   luego _____

llueve _____   noche _____

2. computadora _____   **4.** verde _____

pizarrón _____   ñame _____

escritorio _____   reloj _____

corto _____   ¿qué? _____

¡A DIVERTIRSE!   Nombre _____

Busca las palabras secretas

In each box there is one word that does not belong. Find the word and circle it. Then write the words in the blanks below to make a sentence.

1.

negro	rojo	amarillo
azul	rosado	perro
blanco	morado	verde

2.

loro	canario	tigre
ratón	pez	oso
gris	mariposa	pájaro

El _____ es _____ .

Now draw a picture to illustrate the secret animal.

¿Cómo se dice?

Nombre _____

A. Look at this calendar and answer the questions.

lunes	martes	miércoles	jueves	viernes	sábado	domingo
		1	2	3	4	5
6	7	8	9	10	11	12
13	14	15	16	17	18	19
20	21	22	23	24	25	26
27	28	29	30	31		

M ¿Qué día es el dos? _____ **Es jueves.** _____

1. ¿Qué día es el primero? _____

2. ¿Qué día es el siete? _____

3. ¿Qué día es el diez? _____

4. ¿Qué día es el vientiséis? _____

5. ¿Qué día es el treinta? _____

B. Here are all the days of the week. Divide them into two groups: *días de la semana* and *fines de semana.* Underline *días de la semana* in green, and *fines de semana* in blue.

lunes   sábado   viernes   jueves   martes   miércoles   domingo

¿Cómo se dice?   Nombre _____

A. Your friend always has his head in the clouds, and doesn't know what day he's living in. Look at the calendar in Exercise A and answer his questions about whether dates are *esta semana* or *la próxima semana.* Pretend that today is the 15th.

M ¿Cuándo es el día dieciséis? _____ **esta semana** _____

1. ¿Cuando es el día veintiuno? _____

2. ¿Cuando es el día diecisiete? _____

3. ¿Cuando es el día veinticuatro? _____

4. ¿Cuando es el día diecinueve? _____

5. ¿Cuando es el día veintiséis? _____

¡Piénsalo! ᘡᘡᘡᘡᘡᘡᘡᘡᘡᘡᘡᘡᘡᘡᘡ

What day comes before each of these days?

1. lunes _____

2. sábado _____

3. jueves _____

4. domingo _____

Nombre _____

B. Señorita Durango is from Argentina. She is very interested in the activities of students in North America. How do you answer her questions? Write an answer that is true for you.

M ¿Adónde vas los lunes?

Voy a la escuela los lunes. _____

1. ¿Cuándo vas a la escuela?

_____

2. ¿Adónde vas los fines de semana?

_____

3. ¿Cuándo vas a la casa de un amigo o de una amiga?

_____

4. ¿Vas a la tienda los sábados?

_____

5. ¿Adónde vas la próxima semana?

_____

6. ¿Vas al parque los miércoles?

_____

Nombre _____

C. Miguel has given you a copy of his schedule for this week. What questions can you ask him about his activities? Read Miguel's calendar. Write six questions you could ask him: three questions with *¿Adónde vas?* and three questions with *¿Cuándo vas?* Look at the questions in Exercise A if you need help.

El calendario de Miguel

lunes	martes	miércoles	jueves	viernes	sábado	domingo
la escuela y la clase de piano	la escuela	¡No hay clases! el cine: <<Los flamencos de Miami>>	la escuela y la clase de piano	la escuela y la casa de Inés	la casa de Paco y el parque	la casa y el cine: <<El tigre grande>>

1. _____

2. _____

3. _____

4. _____

5. _____

6. _____

¿Cómo se dice?

Nombre _____

A. Poor Lupita has a cold and can't hear well. Show her what each person is saying by completing the sentence that goes with the picture. Use *a la* or *al*.

M  Voy _____ **a la** _____ escuela.

1.  ¿Vas _____ parque?

2.  ¿Vas _____ cine?

3.  Voy _____ casa.

4.  Voy _____ tienda.

¿Cómo se dice?

Nombre _____

A. You are trying to plan your activities for the week. How do your friends answer your questions? Write *voy, vas,* or *va* in the blank to complete the answer.

M ¿Va Jaime a la escuela hoy?

Sí, Jaime _____**va**_____ a la escuela.

1. ¿Vas a la escuela el martes?

Sí, _____ a la escuela.

2. ¿Va Isabel al cine esta semana?

No, no _____ al cine.

3. ¿Voy a la escuela el domingo?

No, no _____ a la escuela.

4. ¿Va Luis al salón de clase?

Sí, _____ al salón de clase.

5. ¿Vas a la escuela el sábado?

No, no _____ a la escuela.

B. Where are your classmates going? Choose a question to ask three classmates, and then ask them the question. Write a sentence about each person's answer.

Preguntas

1. ¿Vas al cine esta semana?
2. ¿Vas a la clase hoy?
3. ¿Vas a la tienda el fin de semana?

M Tú: ¿Vas al cine esta semana?

José: No, no voy al cine esta semana.

José no va al cine esta semana.

1. _____

2. _____

3. _____

¡A leer!

Nombre _____

Read the paragraph about calendars and do the activities below.

¿Qué es el calendario?

El calendario es una lista de los días del año, con meses y semanas. En el calendario ves qué día es ayer, hoy, mañana o el primero de junio del año 2010. ¡Están los días del pasado, del presente y del futuro!

Usa el calendario para planear el futuro: adónde vas la próxima semana, cuándo vas al cine o cuándo vas de vacaciones a Disneylandia. . . El reloj también mide el tiempo (en horas, minutos y segundos).

> Nota:
> **El pasado** means "the past."
> **Ves** means "you see."
> **Mide el tiempo** means "measures time."

Circle verdadero (true) or falso (false).

1. El calendario es una lista de relojes.   verdadero   falso

2. Los días del año están (are) en el calendario.   verdadero   falso

3. La próxima semana es el futuro.   verdadero   falso

4. El calendario no mide el tiempo.   verdadero   falso

Join the two terms that go together.

ayer   futuro

mañana   presente

hoy   pasado

Nombre _____

Conexión con los estudios sociales

Make your own calendar for this month. Use the blank calendar below. Write the days on the top row, and the numbers in the blanks. Then, color the days according to these instructions.

verde = los fines de semana   rojo = hoy
azul = los días de clase   morado = mañana

Include any holidays or special events in your calendar, such as Halloween, Thanksgiving, or a school Talent Show.

Write each holiday and the date below:

Halloween   martes 31

_____   _____

_____   _____

_____   _____

⸙ ¡APRENDE MÁS! ⸙   Nombre _____

Using the glossary or word list in a textbook is like using a dictionary. It has information to help you find the meaning of a word.

gracias thank you, thanks (B)
grande big, large (2)
la gripe flu (7)
    Tengo la gripe. I have the flu. (7)
gris gray (2)
guapo, guapa good-looking (10)
gustar to like (5)
    Le gusta el verano. He/She likes summer. (5)
    Me gusta la primavera. I like spring. (5)
    ¿Qué te gusta hacer? What do you like to do? (6)
    ¿Te gusta pintar? Do you like to paint? (5)

hay (inf.: haber) there is, there are (1)
    ¿Cuántos . . . hay? How many . . . are there? (1)
    ¿Qué hay . . . ? What is there . . . ?
la hermana sister (10)
la hermanastra stepsister (10)
el hermanastro stepbrother (10)
el hermano brother (10)
los hermanos brothers, brothers and sisters (10)
la hija daughter (10)

Find the following information in your textbook's Spanish-English Word List.

1. What is the first word on page 258 that means "a place to sit"? _____

2. On page 252, what does the abbreviation (m.) mean after the

   word **el arte?** _____

3. What animal's name is on page 260? _____

4. What day of the week is on page 250? _____

5. How many days of the week can you find on page 257? _____

6. What words on page 253 are places? _____

   _____

7. Read page 255, then write down the unit in which the word **el hijo**

   is taught. _____

8. What is the last expression on page 255 that describes the weather?

   _____

 **¡A DIVERTIRSE!** Nombre _____

Un juego de los días

Write the missing days of the week in the squares. One day is already written for you. Use the letters as clues to fill in the other days.

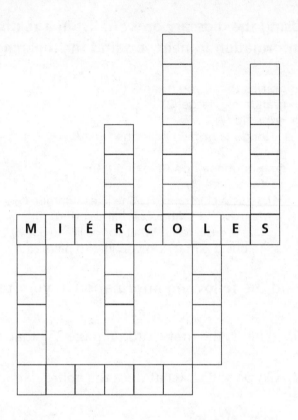

M | I | É | R | C | O | L | E | S

¿Adónde va el maestro?

First fill in the missing letter of each word. Then, complete the sentence by writing the word that is formed by the letters in the boxes.

I N E
M R T E S
J U E V E
D Í

El maestro va a la _____.

Nombre _____

A. Some objects in the classroom are out of place. Where do they go? Draw a line from each classroom object on the left to the picture of where it belongs. Then write the name of the picture in the blank. One has been done for you.

M una hoja de papel 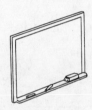 **el cuaderno** _____

unos bolígrafos _____

el reloj  _____

el borrador 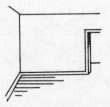 _____

una computadora 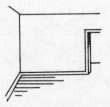 _____

Nombre _____

B. **How many are there? Read the sentence and the question. Then write the answer.**

M Hay diez mesas largas y tres mesas cortas. ¿Cuántas mesas hay?

Hay trece mesas. _____

1. Hay dos canarios y veinte loros. ¿Cuántos pájaros hay?

_____

2. Hay cinco cuadrados blancos, cinco cuadrados azules y cinco cuadrados verdes. ¿Cuántos cuadrados hay?

_____

3. Hay una pared blanca, una pared amarilla y dos paredes rosadas. ¿Cuántas paredes hay?

_____

4. Hay diez gatos, siete perros y once peces. ¿Cuántos animales hay?

_____

5. Hay diez hombres grandes y cuatro hombres pequeños. ¿Cuántos hombres hay?

_____

6. Hay once maestros y quince maestras. ¿Cuántos maestros hay?

_____

Nombre _____

C. Help Consuelo decorate the bulletin board! Find the picture that matches each sentence. Write the letter of the picture on the line beside the sentence. The first one has been done for you. (Look carefully! There are more pictures than there are sentences.)

M Hay un calendario en la pared.   _____ i _____

1. El niño va al cine.   _____

2. La alumna va a la escuela.   _____

3. Hay dos ratones en el pupitre.   _____

4. Hay una mariposa en la ventana.   _____

5. Hay una computadora en el pupitre.   _____

a.
d.
g.
j.

b.
e.
h.
k.

c.
f.
i.
l.

Nombre _____

D. Imagine that you are listening to one side of a telephone conversation. You can hear the answers but not the questions. Choose a question that goes with each answer and write it on the line. There are more questions than answers, so choose carefully!

¿Cuándo vas al parque?   ¿Qué día es hoy?

¿Cuál es tu animal favorito?   ✓ ¿Cómo te llamas?

¿Cómo estás?   ¿Adónde vas el viernes?

¿De qué color es tu perro?   ¿Cuándo vas a la escuela?

¿Cómo es la escuela?   ¿De qué color es el gato?

¿Cuál es tu número de teléfono?   ¿Cuál es tu día favorito?

M P: **¿Cómo te llamas?** _____

    R: Me llamo Patricio.

1. P: _____

    R: Bien, gracias.

2. P: _____

    R: Hoy es sábado.

3. P: _____

    R: Voy al parque el domingo.

4. P: _____

    R: Voy a la escuela el lunes.

5. P: _____

    R: La escuela es grande.

Nombre _____

6. P: _____

R: Mi animal favorito es el gato.

7. P: _____

R: El gato es gris, blanco y marrón.

8. P: _____

R: Mi número de teléfono es el tres, veinte, quince, cero, uno.

¡Piénsalo!

1. Name three classroom objects you can hold in your hand.

_____   _____   _____

2. Write a number from 1 to 4 next to each animal. Rank the animals from the smallest (1) to the largest (4).

_____ conejo   _____ mariposa   _____ tigre   _____ pez

3. Write the names of five animals that can fly.

_____   _____

_____   _____

_____

4. Write an addition problem whose answer is your age.

_____ + _____ = _____

Nombre _____

E. The local movie theater is taking a survey to find out about people who go to the movies. How do you answer the questions? Write answers that are true for you. Try to write complete sentences.

Cine Popular

1. ¿Cómo te llamas? _____

2. ¿Cuál es tu número de teléfono? _____

3. ¿Qué día es hoy? _____

4. ¿Vas al cine hoy? _____

5. ¿Vas al cine esta semana? _____

6. ¿Vas al cine la próxima semana? _____

_____

7. ¿Vas al cine los fines de semana? _____

_____

8. Generalmente, ¿qué día de la semana vas al cine? _____

_____

9. ¿Vas al cine con un amigo o con una amiga? _____

_____

10. ¿Cómo se llama tu amigo o tu amiga? _____

_____

¿Cómo se dice?   Nombre _____

A. Where is Amalia going today? Find the name of the class or place and write it on the lines beside the picture. (Be alert! There are more places than pictures.)

la clase de música   el cine
la clase de computadoras   la clase de arte
la biblioteca   ✓ la escuela
el gimnasio   la casa

M

la escuela

3.

_____

1.

_____

4.

_____

2.

_____

5.

_____

¿Cómo se dice?   Nombre _____

A. Your computer has a mysterious virus which doesn't let you see vowels! Fill in the missing letters on the labels beside each picture. One word has been done for you.

1.    __u_s_a_r l_a_ c_o_mp_u_t_a_d_o_r_a_

2.    tr___b___j___r

3.    ___st___d___r

4.    h___bl___r

5.    pr___ct___c___r d___p___rt___s

6.    p___nt___r

7.    p___rt___c___p___r

8.    ___sc___ch___r

Nombre _____

B. Gregorio has written a paragraph about school. When he didn't know a word, he drew a picture. Help him write the words on the lines below. The first one has been done for you.

Los lunes, los miércoles y los viernes voy a (**M**)

Voy a **(1)** . No voy a **(2)**  . El martes voy al gimnasio

para **(3)** . El jueves voy a **(4)** en **(5)**  .

También voy a cantar en **(6)**  . Voy a **(7)** música también.

M _____**la biblioteca**_____

1. _____

2. _____

3. _____

4. _____

5. _____

6. _____

7. _____

¿Cómo se dice?

Nombre _____

A. You and your friend are playing a guessing game! Read the questions and answer based on the pictures.

M    ¿Qué voy a hacer?

Vas a pintar. _____

1.    ¿Qué va a hacer Marina?

_____

2.    ¿Qué voy a hacer?

_____

3.    ¿Qué vas a hacer?

_____

4.    ¿Qué voy a hacer?

_____

5.    ¿Qué va a hacer Sara?

_____

Nombre _____

B. Hortensia has written you a note about what she and her friend are going to do on Saturday. She wrote it so quickly that she forgot some words! To complete the note, write the appropriate form of *ir a.*

¡Hola! ¿Cómo estás?

El sábado Ⓜ _____voy a_____ ir al cine. Mi amiga Olga

(1) _____ ir al cine también.

Olga (2) _____ estudiar el sábado. El sábado yo

no (3) _____ estudiar. No (4) _____ ir a

la biblioteca.

¿Qué (5) _____ hacer tú el sábado?

(6) ¿_____ ir al cine con unos amigos?

¡Hasta luego!

Hortensia

¿Cómo se dice?

Nombre _____

A. You took a picture of señora Jimenez's study group. Now you have to write captions for the picture. Answer the questions below.

M ¿Qué hace Óscar?   Óscar canta. _____

1. ¿Qué hace Julio?   _____

2. ¿Qué hace Elena?   _____

3. ¿Qué hace Lidia?   _____

4. ¿Qué hace Rósíta?   _____

5. ¿Qué hace Tomás?   _____

6. ¿Qué hace Carlos?   _____

Nombre _____

B. You want to be a reporter someday. You need to practice asking questions. First, read the words to form the question. Then read the answer.

M P: Eduardo / estudiar / dónde

¿Dónde estudia Eduardo? _____

R: Eduardo estudia en el salón de clase.

1. P: Nélida / cantar / cuándo

_____

R: Nélida canta los domingos.

2. P: el señor López / pintar / dónde

_____

R: El señor López pinta en la casa.

3. P: Minerva / participa / dónde

_____

R: Minerva participa en la clase de música.

4. P: la señora Ruiz / deportes / practicar / dónde

_____

R: La señora Ruiz practica deportes en el gimnasio.

Nombre _____

C. Señor Rodríguez thinks that everyone has a special talent. How will you fill
out his questionnaire? Write an answer that is true for you.

M ¿Practicas deportes en la escuela?

Sí, practico deportes en la escuela.
_____

1. ¿Estudias con un amigo o una amiga?

_____

2. ¿Escuchas música en la casa?

_____

3. ¿Pintas en la escuela? ¿Dónde?

_____

4. ¿Cantas muy bien?

_____

5. ¿Hablas por teléfono con un amigo o una amiga?

_____

6. ¿Trabajas en la escuela?

_____

7. ¿Usas una computadora? ¿Dónde?

_____

8. ¿Participas mucho en clase?

_____

¡A leer!

Nombre _____

Read the paragraph about music and choose the best answer.

La música

Las personas cantan, bailan e inventan melodías y canciones. Por eso, hay muchos músicos. Los músicos son personas que tocan música con instrumentos musicales.

Las cosas que se usan para hacer música se llaman instrumentos musicales, como los pianos, los violines, las trompetas, las guitarras y las flautas.

Los músicos van a bailes, fiestas y aniversarios. Escuchas música en el parque, en el cine, en la radio, en la televisión y en las tiendas.

1. ¿Qué hace un músico? _____
   a. toca música
   b. va a clase de música
   c. practica deportes

2. ¿Qué usan los músicos para

   tocar? _____
   a. las clases
   b. el pizarrón
   c. los instrumentos

3. ¿Adónde van los músicos? _____
   a. a las bibliotecas, las clases
      y los gimnasios
   b. a los bailes, las fiestas y los
      aniversarios
   c. a los cines, la televisión y
      las tiendas

Escribe cinco instrumentos musicales.

_____

_____

_____

_____

_____

Nombre _____

Conexión con las matemáticas

Look at the picture. Match each activity with the fraction of students who are doing it. (Be alert! One fraction may match more than one activity.)

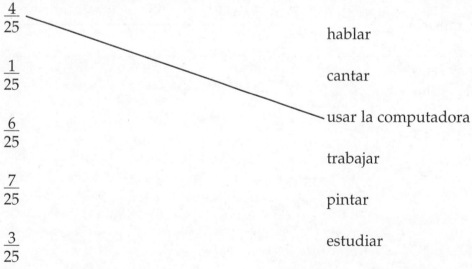

$\dfrac{4}{25}$ hablar

$\dfrac{1}{25}$ cantar

$\dfrac{6}{25}$ usar la computadora

$\dfrac{7}{25}$ trabajar

    pintar

$\dfrac{3}{25}$ estudiar

¡APRENDE MÁS!

Nombre _____

Using a dictionary or glossary is helpful when you can't figure out the meaning of a word. However, many times you can guess the meaning.

Some words in Spanish are similar to words in English. These words are called cognates. Usually, cognates are words that come from the same language. For example, many words in Spanish and English come from Latin, which was spoken by the ancient Romans. Look at the examples below.

Latin	English	Spanish
musica	music	música
studere	study	estudiar

You can often guess the meanings of cognates from the way they are spelled or the way they sound. Read the sentences below and circle the words that are cognates of words in English. Then write the English words on the blanks.

1. El oso polar es blanco y grande.

_____

2. La violeta es una flor morada.

_____

3. La computadora pequeña es moderna.

_____

4. La clase de historia es interesante.

_____

 **¡A DIVERTIRSE!**    **Nombre** _____

Un crucigrama

First, read the sentences and fill in the missing words. Then, write the words in the crossword puzzle.

1. Uso _____ computadoras.

2. Voy a pintar _____ mariposas.

3. Hay _____ gatos en la ventana.

4. Uso _____ lápices cuando estudio.

5. Canto el lunes, el martes, el jueves y el sábado. Canto _____ días.

6. Dieciséis más _____ es veintidós.

7. Hay dos tigres en mi casa. Hay uno en la ventana y hay _____ en el escritorio.

8. Voy a estudiar _____ libros.

9. Hay _____ banderas.

10. Hay _____ peces.

¿Cómo se dice?   Nombre _____

A. What kinds of weather occur in each season? Using colored pencils or crayons, draw a line from the season to the weather that happens in that season. You may draw more than one line from a season to its weather. Look at the list and use the right color for each season.

la primavera = verde   el verano = anaranjado

el invierno = negro   el otoño = rojo

la primavera

el invierno

el verano

el otoño

B. Now answer each question below by naming the kinds of weather you connected to each season.

M ¿Qué tiempo hace en el verano?   **En el verano hace sol y hace calor.**

1. ¿Qué tiempo hace en el otoño? _____

2. ¿Qué tiempo hace en el invierno? _____

3. ¿Qué tiempo hace en la primavera? _____

¿Cómo se dice?

Nombre _____

A. When the seasons change, the weather can be different each day of the week! Fill in the calendar with the right type of weather, and then use the calendar to answer the questions.

Nieva.   Está nublado.   Hace sol.   Hace frío.
Llueve.   Hace calor.   Hace viento.

lunes	martes	miércoles	jueves	viernes	sábado	domingo
						Hace
_____	_____	_____	_____	_____	_____	**frío.**
_____	_____	_____	_____		_____	

M ¿Qué tiempo hace el domingo?

Hace frío. _____

1. ¿Qué tiempo hace el miércoles?

_____

4. ¿Qué tiempo hace el viernes?

_____

2. ¿Qué tiempo hace el sábado?

_____

5. ¿Qué tiempo hace el martes?

_____

3. ¿Qué tiempo hace el lunes?

_____

6. ¿Qué tiempo hace el jueves?

_____

¿Cómo se dice?   Nombre _____

A. The class newspaper must be ready by tomorrow, but you haven't interviewed Alberto Suárez, the student of the week! Complete the questions you ask. Then complete Alberto's answer.

M P: ¿_____ **Te gusta** _____ el verano?

R: Sí, _____ **me gusta** _____ mucho el verano.

1. P: ¿_____ la clase de arte?

R: No pinto bien. No _____ la clase de arte.

2. P: ¿_____ el gimnasio?

R: Es muy grande. Sí, _____ mucho.

3. P: ¿_____ ir a la biblioteca?

R: No estudio mucho. No _____ ir a la biblioteca.

Nombre _____

B. Now that you've finished your interview with Alberto Suárez, write the story for the newspaper. Go back to the interview if you need to.

El alumno de la semana: Alberto Suárez

El alumno de la semana se llama Alberto Suárez. Es alumno de la escuela Bolívar. La estación favorita de Alberto es el verano. A Alberto ___le gusta mucho___ el verano.

Alberto no pinta bien. No _____.

El gimnasio es muy grande. Alberto practica deportes en el gimnasio. A Alberto

_____.

Alberto no estudia mucho. No _____.

C. Imagine that you have been chosen student of the week. Luckily, you can write your own story. Write eight sentences. Write four using *me gusta* and four using *no me gusta.*

_____

_____

_____

_____

_____

_____

¿Cómo se dice?

Nombre _____

A. You are in the pet shop, picking a new pet for yourself. Nuria, the assistant, wants to know what animals you prefer. Write your answers. Then, color the animals in the color you picked.

M ¿Te gusta el pez rojo o el pez anaranjado?

Me gusta el rojo. *or* **Me gusta el anaranjado.**

1. ¿Te gusta el conejo negro o el marrón?

2. ¿Te gusta el canario amarillo o el verde?

3. ¿Te gusta el loro verde o el azul?

4. ¿Te gusta el gato negro o el gato gris?

Nombre _____

B. Your partner left his backpack at home! But he doesn't need to worry, because you can lend him what he wants. Unscramble the sentences and write them in the correct order. Then ask your partner the questions and write what he or she answers.

M ¿gusta, te el bolígrafo o el verde rojo el Cuál?

¿Cuál te gusta, el bolígrafo rojo o el verde?

1. ¿el cuaderno, Cuál o pequeño el gusta te grande?

_____

_____

2. ¿la Cuál te gusta, larga o la corta regla?

_____

_____

3. ¿te el lápiz Cuál negro el o gusta, blanco?

_____

_____

4. ¿Cuál gusta, gordo te o el flaco el perro?

_____

_____

¡A leer!

Nombre _____

Read the letter that Tina wrote to her cousin Sonia.

Los planes de Tina

Querida Sonia:
  Esta semana voy a hacer muchas cosas. Los planes dependen del tiempo.
  El jueves voy al cine. Pero si hace sol, voy al parque.
  El viernes, si hace buen tiempo, voy a practicar deportes. Si hace mal tiempo, voy a estudiar y a usar la computadora.
  El sábado, si está lloviendo me quedo en casa. Si no llueve, voy a la casa de una amiga.
  El domingo, si hace frío voy a patinar sobre hielo. Si hace sol, voy a pintar en el parque con Raúl.
  ¿Qué vas a hacer tú?

Tu amiga,
Tina

Nota:
Si (without a written accent) means *if*.
Pero means *but*.
Hielo means *ice*.

This is the weather for the days Tina has plans. Say what Tina will do on each day, according to her letter.

M El jueves hace sol. <u>Tina va al parque.</u>

1. El viernes hace mal tiempo. _____

2. El sábado no llueve. _____

3. El domingo hace frio. _____

Nombre _____

Conexión con el arte

Seasons and colors can both affect your mood. Seasons can be closely associated with some colors, although this depends on where you live! What colors do you associate with each season? Write them in Spanish.

la primavera: _____

el verano: _____

el otoño: _____

el invierno: _____

Now pick your favorite season and draw a postcard to show it. Draw things that remind you of that season. Use the colors you associate with that time of year.

 **¡APRENDE MÁS!**

Nombre _____

Word lists and dictionaries give you more information about words than just a definition. Sometimes that information is abbreviated. Look at the following abbreviations in English. (These are the same abbreviations that appear on page 251 of your textbook.)

adj.   adjective
adv.   adverb
com.   command
f.   feminine

inf.   infinitive
m.   masculine
pl.   plural
s.   singular

Use the Spanish–English Word List in your textbook to answer the following questions:

1. Is the word ¡Úsalo! an adjective, an adverb, or a command? _____

2. On what page do you find the entry for ¡Úsalo!? _____

3. How many abbreviations follow the word ¡Úsalo!? _____

4. What are the abbreviations after ¡Úsalo!? _____

5. In an exercise titled ¡Úsalo!, what do you do? _____

6. On page 257, find one adverb *(adv.)*. _____

7. What does the adverb on page 257 mean? _____

8. What abbreviation follows the word **marrón?** _____

9. What word do you use to mean many things are **marrón?** _____

¡A DIVERTIRSE!

Nombre _____

Busca las palabras

Read each sentence. Look in the puzzle for the word or words in heavy black letters. Each word may appear across or down in the puzzle. When you find the word, circle it. One has been done for you.

1. **Voy** a la escuela en el **otoño**.

2. **Llueve** en la **primavera**.

3. ¿Qué **tiempo** hace en el **invierno**?

4. Hace **viento** y **hace** mucho **frío**.

5. ¿Hace **sol** en el **verano**?

6. ¿Está **nevando hoy**?

7. Hace **calor** en el verano.

```
O  T  O  Ñ  O  O   S  H  B  T  P
N  U  V  I  E  N   T  O  O  R
E  R  B  S  C  C   H  I  V  I
V  L  E  F  H  A   C  E  E  M
A  L  S  R  O  L   V  O  R  A
N  U  O  Í  P  O   O  R  A  V
D  E  H  O  Y  R   Y  T  N  E
O  V  Y  T  I  E   M  P  O  R
Ñ  E  C  X  V  S   O  L  Ñ  A
I  N  V  I  E  R   N  O  Y  T
```

¿Cómo se dice?

Nombre _____

A. Marcos is proud of himself! He has spelled all the months of the year correctly. Now he wants you to put the months in the correct order. Marcos has already done the first one.

marzo	agosto	febrero	octubre
noviembre	mayo	julio	abril
✓enero	septiembre	diciembre	junio

1. _____ enero _____   7. _____

2. _____   8. _____

3. _____   9. _____

4. _____   10. _____

5. _____   11. _____

6. _____   12. _____

B. What months come right before and right after these months? Write them on the lines.

M _____ enero _____   febrero   _____ marzo _____

1. _____ mayo _____

2. _____ agosto _____

3. _____ noviembre _____

¿Cómo se dice?   Nombre _____

A. Now Marcos wants to write about what he likes and doesn't like to do during the year. He's looking at his pictures from the past year to remember what he usually does and what he enjoys most. Help him complete his report.

En el verano me gusta mucho _____**nadar**_____. En la primavera me

gusta _____ en el parque y en el otoño me gusta

_____ en casa. Pero en el invierno no me gusta

_____. Los fines de semana también son muy divertidos.

Me gusta _____ con mi mamá en casa y también

_____ con unos amigos. Pero no me gusta

_____ en el supermercado. Hay una cosa que no me

gusta nada: _____.

¿Cómo se dice?

Nombre _____

A. What do these children do, and when? Look at the pictures and complete the sentences.

M Susana _____ **nada el siete de noviembre.** _____

_____

1. Martín _____

_____

2. Marta _____

_____

3. Eric _____

_____

B. Do you do the same things as these children? Say *yo también* or *yo no*, according to what you do.

M _Yo también nado el siete de noviembre. (Yo no nado el siete de noviembre.)_

1. _____

2. _____

3. _____

Nombre _____

C. Señor Amable wants to be sure that his park has something for everyone! First, he must find out what people like to do and when they like to do it. How will you fill out his questionnaire? Answer the questions.

¡Un parque para todos!

M ¿Te gusta practicar deportes?

Sí, me gusta practicar deportes. _____

M ¿Cuándo practicas deportes?

Practico deportes en julio y agosto. _____

1. ¿Te gusta patinar?

   _____

2. ¿Cuándo patinas?

   _____

3. ¿Te gusta nadar?

   _____

4. ¿Cuándo nadas?

   _____

5. ¿Te gusta caminar?

   _____

6. ¿Cuándo caminas?

   _____

Nombre _____

D. At the Escuela Buenavista, both students and teachers like to keep busy. Who likes to do each activity? It's hard to tell unless you ask. For each picture, complete the answer by writing *yo, tú, él, ella,* or *usted.*

M  ¿Quién patina? _____**Él**_____ patina.

1. ¿Quién baila? _____ bailo.

2.  ¿Quién nada? _____ nadas.

3. ¿Quién camina? _____ camina.

4.  ¿Quién canta? _____ canta.

5. ¿Quién estudia? _____ estudia.

Nombre _____

E. Choose a partner. Then find out what your partner does at home. You must make up your questions in advance. Write your partner's answers.

M ¿Usas la computadora en casa? _____

Él o Ella: Sí, yo uso la computadora los fines de semana.

Ella usa la computadora los fines de semana. _____

Preguntas

1. _____

2. _____

3. _____

4. _____

5. _____

Respuestas

1. _____

2. _____

3. _____

4. _____

5. _____

Nombre _____

F. The Payasos are an unusual couple. Señor Payaso is sensible and a little dull. Señora Payaso is wild and sometimes quite silly. You are a reporter who is interviewing the Payasos. Complete each question and record their answer.

M  P: Señor Payaso, ¿quién patina en la casa,

_____**usted**_____ o _____**ella**_____?

R: ___**Ella patina en la casa. Yo no patino.**___

1. P: Señora Payaso, ¿quién canta en la biblioteca,

_____ o _____?

R: _____

2.  P: Señor Payaso, ¿quién usa la computadora,

_____ o _____?

R: _____

3. P: Señora Payaso, ¿quién nada en enero,

_____ o _____?

R: _____

4.  P: Señor Payaso, ¿quién baila en la mesa,

_____ o _____?

R: _____

¿Cómo se dice?

Nombre _____

A. To help you with your reporting job, Francisco showed you part of his schedule. Complete the sentences with *siempre, a veces,* or *nunca.*

L	M	M	J	V	S	D
a	a	a	a	a	b	
d	b	b	b	c		
a	a	a	a	a	b	d
d			d	c		
a	a	a	a	a	b	
	b	b				

a = ir a la escuela
b = practicar deportes
c = cantar en la clase de música
d = usar la computadora

M _____Siempre_____ va a la escuela los miércoles.

1. _____ practica deportes los miércoles.

2. _____ canta en la clase de música los domingos.

3. _____ usa la computadora los martes.

4. _____ practica deportes los sábados.

B. What do you like to do in your spare time? Complete the questions in this survey by using *siempre, a veces,* or *nunca.* Fill it out with your own answers.

M ¿_____Siempre_____ estudias en casa?

Sí, siempre estudio en casa.

2. ¿_____ usas la computadora en agosto?

_____

1. ¿_____ patinas en el invierno?

_____

3. ¿_____ nadas en diciembre?

_____

¡A leer!

Nombre _____

Read the text and fill out the chart.

Lo contrario

Las estaciones son diferentes en los dos hemisferios del mundo. Por ejemplo, si en Estados Unidos hace frío, en Argentina hace calor. Si en Argentina hace frío, en Estados Unidos hace calor. Si en Estados Unidos es el invierno, en Argentina es el verano. ¡Si en Argentina es la primavera, en Estados Unidos es el otoño!

Los meses de las estaciones también son diferentes. En Estados Unidos el invierno es en diciembre, enero y febrero. La primavera es en marzo, abril y mayo. El verano es en junio, julio y agosto. El otoño es en septiembre, octubre y noviembre. ¡Pero en Argentina es exactamente lo contrario!

Nota:
Hemisferio means *hemisphere*.
Estados Unidos means *United States*.
Lo contrario means *the opposite*.

Fill out the chart with the months for each season in each country. Remember that they are the opposite.

	Estados Unidos	Argentina
invierno	diciembre, enero, febrero	
verano		
primavera		
otoño		

Conexión con la cultura

In Spanish-speaking countries, children love to play. They play in their schoolyard, in the streets and inside their homes. Most of the games they play you probably know, but with different names. Look at the pictures and try to write the correct names of the games in Spanish. Use a dictionary if you need it.

la rayuela   las canicas   el trompo   el escondite   ✓ la mancha

la mancha _____

_____

_____

_____

_____

Do you play these games too? Write sentences using *También me gusta* or *No me gusta*.

Ⓜ También me gusta jugar a la mancha. *or* No me gusta jugar a la mancha.
_____

1. _____

2. _____

3. _____

4. _____

 ¡APRENDE MÁS!

Nombre _____

The names of the months in most of Europe and America all come from the calendar created in ancient Rome-the Julian calendar. The Julian calendar was not perfect, and so it was revised in the sixteenth century. The new, improved calendar was called the Gregorian calendar. Although the calendar was improved, the names of the months stayed the same.

The lists below are in five different languages: English, French, German, Italian, and Spanish. Study the lists and guess which language each list is in. Write the letter of the list on the blank beside the name of the language. (Two of them should be very easy for you!)

a	b	c	d	e
janvier	Januar	enero	gennaio	January
février	Februar	febrero	febbraio	February
mars	März	marzo	marzo	March
avril	April	abril	aprile	April
mai	Mai	mayo	maggio	May
juin	Juni	junio	giugno	June
juillet	Juli	julio	luglio	July
août	August	agosto	agosto	August
septembre	September	septiembre	settembre	September
octobre	Oktober	octubre	ottobre	October
novembre	November	noviembre	novembre	November
décembre	Dezember	diciembre	dicembre	December

_____ English   _____ German   _____ Spanish

_____ French   _____ Italian

 **¡A DIVERTIRSE!**   Nombre _____

Una frase feliz

Complete each sentence with a word from the box. Then use the numbers to discover the secret phrase.

✓año	octubre	nadar	patinar
gusta	voy	enero	agosto

1. Doce meses son un $\underset{1}{\text{a}}$ $\underset{2}{\text{ñ}}$ $\underset{3}{\text{o}}$.

2. Me gusta $\underset{4\ \ \ \ 5\ \ \ \ 6\ \ \ \ 7\ \ \ \ 8}{\rule{2.5cm}{0.4pt}}$ en el verano.

3. Llueve y hace viento en $\underset{9\ \ \ 10\ \ \ 11\ \ \ 12\ \ \ 13\ \ \ 14\ \ \ 15}{\rule{3.5cm}{0.4pt}}$.

4. En $\underset{16\ \ \ 17\ \ \ 18\ \ \ 19\ \ \ 20}{\rule{2.5cm}{0.4pt}}$ nieva y hace frío.

5. En $\underset{21\ \ \ 22\ \ \ 23\ \ \ 24\ \ \ 25\ \ \ 26}{\rule{3cm}{0.4pt}}$ hace sol y hace calor.

6. No $\underset{27\ \ \ 28\ \ \ 29}{\rule{1.5cm}{0.4pt}}$ a la escuela en el verano.

7. A María le gusta $\underset{30\ \ \ 31\ \ \ 32\ \ \ 33\ \ \ 34\ \ \ 35\ \ \ 36}{\rule{3.5cm}{0.4pt}}$ en febrero.

8. A Natán le $\underset{37\ \ \ 38\ \ \ 39\ \ \ 40\ \ \ 41}{\rule{2.5cm}{0.4pt}}$ bailar siempre.

What do you say on New Year's Day?

¡P $\underset{8\ \ \ 23\ \ \ 39\ \ \ 30\ \ \ 16\ \ \ 36\ \ \ 3}{\rule{3.5cm}{0.4pt}}$ $\underset{7\ \ \ 2\ \ \ 28}{\rule{1.5cm}{0.4pt}}$ $\underset{17\ \ \ 38\ \ \ 15\ \ \ 27\ \ \ 9}{\rule{2.5cm}{0.4pt}}$!

Nombre _____

A. The students in señora Lozano's class are daydreaming while they wait for the cafeteria line to move. Complete each sentence according to the picture.

M A Zoraida le gusta el verano. _____

1. A Alberto _____

2. A Rosita _____

3. A Juan _____

4. A Ramón _____

5. A Arturo _____

Nombre _____

B. You are participating in a survey of student likes and dislikes. You're asked to complete this chart. You have to choose the answer that comes closest to how you feel.

M Me gusta. . .
   a. estudiar.
   b. pintar.
   ©. cantar.

1. Me gusta mucho. . .
   a. el invierno.
   b. el otoño.
   c. la primavera.
   d. el verano.

2. No me gusta. . .
   a. practicar deportes.
   b. cantar.
   c. estudiar.
   d. pintar.

3. Me gusta. . .
   a. ir al cine.
   b. ir a la biblioteca.
   c. ir a la escuela.
   d. ir al gimnasio.

4. No me gusta. . .
   a. la clase de arte.
   b. la clase de música.
   c. el gimnasio.
   d. la clase de computadoras.

Now, what questions would you ask a friend to find out if he likes the same things as you do? Write them down according to the things you marked above.

M ¿Te gusta cantar? _____

1. _____

2. _____

3. _____

4. _____

5. _____

Nombre _____

C. At summer camp, Elena Bosque is planning activities. First, she needs to know what people do. Complete each answer with the correct pronoun.

M ¿Quién camina mucho, tú o Alfredo?

_____**Él**_____ camina mucho.

1. ¿Quién nada muy bien, Miguel o tú?

_____ nado muy bien.

2. Señora Elías, ¿quién pinta muy bien, usted o Alicia?

_____ pinta muy bien.

3. Enrique, ¿quién camina mucho, tú o yo?

_____ caminas mucho.

4. ¿Quién canta muy bien, tú o Federico?

_____ canta muy bien.

D. Now Elena wants to know what you do. What are her questions? Write them on the blanks.

M ¿/ practicar / deportes / ?

¿Practicas deportes?
_____

1. ¿ / caminar / mucho /?

_____

2. ¿ / pintar / muy / bien / ?

_____

3. ¿ / cantar / muy / bien / ?

_____

4. ¿ / bailar / mucho / ?

_____

Nombre _____

E. Imagine that this is Rita's calendar of after-school activities. How does Rita answer your questions? Use the calendar to answer the questions as if you were Rita.

lunes	martes	miércoles	jueves	viernes
la clase de trompeta y estudiar	la casa de Ana y bailar	el gimnasio y practicar deportes	la clase de trompeta y estudiar	el cine y caminar—la casa de Luis

M ¿Adónde vas el jueves?

Voy a la clase de trompeta. _____

1. ¿Adónde vas el viernes?

_____

2. ¿Qué vas a hacer el miércoles?

_____

3. ¿Adónde vas el martes?

_____

4. ¿Adónde vas el miércoles?

_____

5. ¿Qué vas a hacer el viernes?

_____

Nombre _____

F. Little Paquito is curious about Rita's activities, too. How do you answer Paquito's questions? Use the calendar on page 88 to check Rita's schedule and write your answers.

M ¿Qué hace Rita el jueves?

Va a la clase de trompeta y estudia.

1. ¿Qué hace Rita el viernes?

   _____

2. ¿Qué hace Rita el lunes?

   _____

3. ¿Qué hace Rita el miércoles?

   _____

4. ¿Qué hace Rita el martes?

   _____

¡Piénsalo! ~~~~~~~~~~~~~~~~~~~~~~~

The pet shop is about to close. Make a decision about which animal you like better.

   ¿Cuál te gusta, la tortuga grande o la pequeña?

   _____

   ¿Cuál te gusta, el lagarto largo o el corto?

   _____

Nombre _____

G. How well do you know yourself? How well do you know your classmate? Take the following quiz. First answer according to what you like. Then answer according to what you think your classmate likes. Compare answers with your classmate to find out if you were right.

M ¿Qué bolígrafo te gusta?

Me gusta el largo. Le gusta el corto. *or* **Le gusta el largo.**

_____

1. ¿Qué gato te gusta?

_____

_____

2. ¿Qué casa te gusta?

_____

_____

3. ¿Qué mariposa te gusta?

_____

_____

4. ¿Qué loro te gusta?

_____

_____

¿Cómo se dice?   Nombre _____

A. Try this guessing game. What do the pictures make you think of? Answer the question ¿*Qué tienes*?

Ⓜ [image]

Tengo sed. _____

2.

_____

1.

_____

3.

_____

B. You are eating in a noisy restaurant. You can only hear part of the conversations around you. Can you guess the questions to the answers you hear?

Ⓜ **¿Tienes hambre?** _____

Sí, tengo hambre. Quiero una hamburguesa.

1. _____

No. No tengo sueño, tengo frío.

2. _____

Sí, tengo sed.

3. _____

¿Karina? Tiene la gripe.

4. _____

¿Yo? Tengo calor.

¿Cómo se dice?

Nombre _____

A. Ignacio is having a hard day. Describe Ignacio's day. Match each sentence to the correct picture.

No tiene razón.

Tiene prisa.

No tiene suerte.

Tiene la gripe.

Tiene miedo.

Tiene hambre.

Tiene frío.

Tiene sueño.

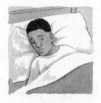

¿Cómo se dice?   Nombre _____

A. You are visiting the Serrano family to play with your friend, Guillermo. Your mom *(tu mamá)* is coming with you. Will you greet them using *tú* or *usted*? Look at the picture and at the greetings, and decide if they are something you could say, your mother could say, or both could say.

	tú	tu mamá
M ¡Hola, Guillermo!	x	x
1. ¿Cómo está usted, doña Margarita?	____	____
2. Hola, Pilar. ¿Cómo estás?	____	____
3. Hola, don Jesús. ¿Cómo está usted?	____	____
4. ¡Don Francisco! ¿Cómo está?	____	____
5. ¿Cómo está, doña Pilar?	____	____

B. It's Talent Night at the community center. What a talented group of people! Use the word in parentheses to complete the sentence saying what each person does well.

M Señorita Vásquez, _____ **usted canta** _____ muy bien. (cantar)

1. Josefina, _____ muy bien. (pintar)

2. Señora Calvo, _____ muy bien. (patinar)

3. Vicente, _____ deportes muy bien. (practicar)

4. Señorita Martínez, _____ muy bien. (nadar)

Nombre _____

C. Beatriz has interviewed many people at her school. You have found her notes. What questions did she ask? Write them on the blanks.

M La señora Trillo patina mucho.

¿Patina usted mucho? _____

1. Estela camina mucho los sábados.

   _____

2. Ricardo usa la computadora en la biblioteca.

   _____

3. El señor Perales nada todos los días.

   _____

4. La señorita Ojeda va al gimnasio los viernes.

   _____

5. Gilberto no practica deportes.

   _____

¡Piénsalo! ∿∿∿∿∿∿∿∿∿∿∿

What would you say if you found a pot of gold? Follow the arrows and write the words in the blanks.

¡__ __ __ __ __ __

__ __ __ __ __ __

__ __ __ __ __ __ __ __ __!

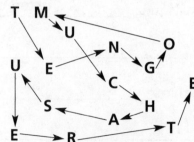

¿Cómo se dice?   Nombre _____

A. Señor Montalvo's class held a rummage sale. What did everyone buy?
Complete and answer the question according to the picture. Use *tengo*,
tienes, or *tiene*.

M P: ¿Qué _____**tiene**_____ Alberto?

R: Él _____**tiene**_____ un oso negro.

1. P: Señor Montalvo, ¿qué _____ usted?

R: _____ un globo grande.

2. P: Elisa, ¿qué _____ tú?

R: _____ un loro.

3. P: ¿Qué _____ Verónica?

R: Ella _____ un calendario.

4. P: Daniel, ¿qué _____ tú?

R: _____ un mapa.

5. P: Señora Vega, ¿qué _____ usted?

R: _____ unos peces.

6. P: ¿Qué _____ Rafael?

R: Él _____ unos libros.

Nombre _____

B. Your friend Juan isn't very good at Spanish! He has described these pictures and has made mistakes in some of them. Luckily, he's got you to help him. Read his sentences and rewrite the ones that are not correct. Careful: Some sentences are correct. Write *correcto* next to the correct sentences.

M Tengo cinco lápices.

_____

1. Él tiene dos gatos.

_____

2. Yo tengo un libro.

_____

3. Yo tengo una computadora.

_____

C. You have discovered an interesting fact: Tomás, Magdalena and you always have ten of everything among the three of you! You are talking to Tomás about this. Complete your sentences.

M Yo tengo tres lápices y Magdalena tiene dos lápices.

Tú tienes cinco lápices.

1. Magdalena tiene cinco libros y tú tienes cuatro libros.

_____

2. Tú tienes tres sillas y yo tengo tres sillas.

_____

3. Yo tengo seis cuadernos y Magdalena no tiene cuadernos.

_____

¡A leer!

Nombre _____

Read the paragraph and answer the questions.

El camello

Un camello camina por el desierto. Tiene calor, pero no tiene sed. Al caminar, piensa. . . "El camino por el desierto siempre es largo. Camino y camino de día y de noche. Días y días, semanas y semanas. . . Voy en la caravana de camellos. Uno, dos, tres, cuatro, veinte camellos vamos en la caravana. No tengo sed. Siempre voy por el desierto, de color amarillo y marrón. Voy al oasis. Me gustan los oasis con palmeras. Las serpientes no me gustan, pero nunca tengo miedo".

> Nota:
> **Camello** means *camel.*
> **Desierto** means *desert.*
> **Camino** means *path.*

1. ¿Cómo es el camino por el desierto?

    El camino por el desierto es largo. _____

2. ¿De qué colores es el desierto?

    _____

3. ¿Adónde va el camello?

    _____

4. ¿Cuántos camellos hay en la caravana?

    _____

5. ¿Qué tiene el camello?

    _____

6. ¿Qué no tiene el camello?

    _____

Nombre _____

Conexión con las matemáticas

Look at this weather report for some cities in Latin America and Spain. What is the temperature there today? Color in the thermometers to indicate the temperature. Decide whether it is cold or hot. Write *Hace frío.* or *Hace calor.* Then look at the icons and describe the weather.

	Temperatura	Tiempo	¿Qué tiempo hace?
Asunción			
Buenos Aires			
Caracas			
La Habana			
La Paz			
Madrid			

Expresa tus ideas

Nombre _____

The Explorers' Club visited the Tropical World exhibit at the zoo. Señorita Aventura took a picture of the members. It's your job to write a story for the club newspaper. Write at least five sentences about the picture.

hay	calor	hambre	grande
hace	dolor	sueño	niños
tener	sed	miedo	niñas

_____

_____

_____

_____

_____

_____

_____

_____

¡A DIVERTIRSE!

Nombre _____

Una nota secreta

Patricia has passed you a note in class. Break the secret code to find out what she is saying. Circle the letters in the note to form words. Then write each letter in order.

```
Ⓣ  I  J  K  E  I  J  K  N  I  J  K

G  I  J  K  O  I  J  K  M  I  J  K

U  I  J  K  C  I  J  K  H  I  J  K

A  I  J  K  H  I  J  K  A  I  J  K

M  I  J  K  B  I  J  K  R  I  J  K

E  I  J  K
```

¿Cómo se dice?   Nombre _____

A. Margarita is impatient. Fifteen minutes seem like an hour to her. Color the clocks to show her when you will do different activities. Note that *en* means in.

M Voy a la escuela en media hora.

1. Voy a estudiar en dos horas.

2. Voy a bailar en un cuarto de hora.

3. Voy a usar la computadora en una hora.

4. Voy a la casa en media hora.

5. Voy a caminar en una hora y cuarto.

¡Piénsalo!

How long do these activities last? Write the answer next to the times.

Nadar el sábado 11:15–11:45 _____ **media hora** _____

Caminar en el parque 12:00–1:30 _____

Clase de música 3:30–4:45 _____

Comprar un libro 5:00–5:15 _____

Comer pizza 8:00–8:30 _____

¿Cómo se dice?

Nombre _____

A. Look at Martín's schedule and complete the dialogues using *por la mañana,* *por la tarde,* or *por la noche.*

M —¿Cuándo vas a la biblioteca, Martín?

—Voy el sábado _____**por la mañana**_____.

1. —Y, ¿cuándo vas al cine?

—Voy el miércoles _____.

2. —¿Cuándo va a la tienda Martín?

—Va el domingo _____.

3. —Martín patina los lunes por la noche.

—No, él patina los jueves _____.

lunes: parque (5:00pm)
miércoles: cine (7:00pm)
jueves: patinar (9:30pm)
sábado: biblioteca (9:00am)
domingo: tienda (10:00am)

B. How observant are you? Look at the pictures and decide at what time of day the activities take place. Write a sentence telling what you decided.

M    **2.**    **4.**

__Es la medianoche.__   _____   _____

1.    **3.**    **5.**

_____   _____   _____

¿Cómo se dice?   Nombre _____

A. Hortensia has made a chart to teach her brother how to tell time. Help her finish the chart. Draw a line from the sentence to the right clock. (Careful! There are too many clocks!)

M Son las ocho en punto.

1. Son las cuatro y cinco.

2. Es la una en punto.

3. Son las siete y cuarto.

4. Son las tres y media.

Nombre _____

B. You should have changed the battery in your watch. It's running five minutes slow. Tell the right time by adding five minutes to the time on the clock. Write a sentence.

 Son las tres y cinco. _____

3. 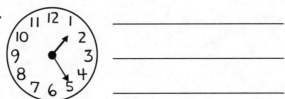 _____

_____

1.  _____

_____

4. 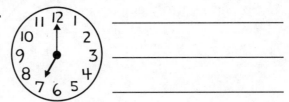 _____

_____

2.  _____

_____

5.  _____

_____

¡Piénsalo!

Ricky wants you to go to the movies with him. Decode his message by unscrambling the letters and writing the words on the lines.

¿A _____ _____ _____ al _____?
   éuq   aohr   avs   enic

Voy a _____ _____ _____ _____.
       lsa   occni   ne   unpto

Nombre _____

C. Manuel has a busy week! Can you help him answer questions about his activities? Use the schedule below.

	por la mañana	por la tarde	por la noche
lunes	9:30–clase de música	3:30–biblioteca	8:00–estudiar en casa
martes	9:40–clase de arte	5:10–dentista	8:30–estudiar en casa
miércoles	10:45–clase de español	4:45–casa de Jorge	7:45–estudiar en casa
jueves	11:15–clase de computadoras	4:30–biblioteca	7:45–estudiar en casa de Jorge
viernes	¡FIESTA!	2:30–nadar	9:30–casa de Ana
sábado	11:00–gimnasio	3:45–tienda	9:00–cine
domingo	11:30–parque	4:15–casa de Ana	8:00–estudiar en casa

M ¿A qué hora vas a ir al cine el sábado?

A las nueve y media de la noche. _____

1. ¿A qué hora vas a ir a clase de música el lunes?

   _____

2. ¿Cuándo vas a ir al gimnasio?

   _____

3. ¿Cuándo vas a ir al dentista?

   _____

4. ¿Qué vas a hacer el viernes por la tarde?

   _____

5. ¿Cuándo vas a ir a casa de Ana?

   _____

6. ¿Qué vas a hacer el lunes y el martes por la noche?

   _____

Nombre _____

D. Bárbara and Berta are best friends. On Saturday, they like to spend a lot of time together. They even made a schedule of their activities. Answer the question according to the schedule.

Bárbara
8:40 / la clase de arte
9:38 / la casa de Berta
11:00 / la casa
3:40 / la biblioteca

Berta
9:30 / la casa
11:00 / la casa de Bárbara
1:20 / la clase de computadoras
3:35 / la biblioteca

M ¿A qué hora va Bárbara a la clase de arte?

Va a la clase de arte a las nueve menos veinte. _____

1. ¿Cuándo va Berta a la casa de Bárbara?

_____

2. ¿Cuándo va Bárbara a la casa de Berta?

_____

3. ¿A qué hora va Berta a la clase de computadoras?

_____

4. ¿A qué hora va Berta a la biblioteca?

_____

5. ¿Cuándo camina Bárbara a la biblioteca?

_____

¿Cómo se dice?

Nombre _____

A. You dropped your note cards and got them all mixed up. Match the questions with the answers by writing the letter of the correct answer next to the question.

1. ¿Cómo te llamas? _____
2. ¿Adónde vas? _____
3. ¿Qué día es hoy? _____
4. ¿Qué es? _____
5. ¿Quién es? _____
6. ¿Qué hora es? _____
7. ¿A qué horas bailas? _____
8. ¿Cuántos lápices hay? _____

a. Es Mariano Huerta.

b. Bailo a las seis y cuarto.

c. Hay cinco lápices.

d. Me llamo Ana López.

e. Voy al cine.

f. Es un pizarrón.

g. Son las seis y cuarto.

h. Es miércoles.

B. Now, ask the above questions to a partner. Write down his or her answers.

_____

_____

_____

_____

_____

_____

Nombre _____

C. You are interviewing a foreign exchange student. Complete your question with the correct question word.

Cuál   Adónde   Quién   A qué hora
Cuándo   Cómo   Dónde   Qué

M Rita: ¿_____**Dónde**_____ estudias los lunes?

Óscar: Estudio en la biblioteca.

1. Rita: ¿_____ vas a la casa por la tarde?

Óscar: Voy a la casa a las cuatro menos veinte.

2. Rita: ¿_____ haces los sábados por la noche?

Óscar: A veces voy al cine los sábados.

3. Rita: ¿_____ es tu animal favorito?

Óscar: Mi animal favorito es el elefante.

4. Rita: ¿_____ son los elefantes?

Óscar: Son grises. Son muy grandes.

D. Write three statements about yourself. Then write three questions you would ask a friend to find out the same information.

Statements   Questions

M ___Tengo muchos amigos.___   **M** ___¿Cuántos amigos tienes?___

1. _____   **1.** _____

2. _____   **2.** _____

3. _____   **3.** _____

¡A leer!

Nombre _____

Read the paragraph and answer the questions.

El tiempo

Un calendario mide el tiempo en días y meses. Un reloj mide el tiempo en horas, minutos y segundos. En un día hay 24 horas, 1,440 minutos y 86,400 segundos. ¡Es mucho tiempo!

Quizás no te gusta tu reloj porque te levantas a la salida del sol. Pero un reloj es importante para saber qué hora es, a qué hora vas a las clases, cuándo estás con tus amigos y por cuánto tiempo. Hay muchos relojes diferentes: digitales, de sol, con alarma, para los deportes, etc.

1. ¿Cómo mide el tiempo un calendario?

_____

2. ¿Cómo mide el tiempo un reloj?

_____

3. ¿Cuántas horas hay en un día?

_____

Dibuja tres tipos diferentes de relojes. ¿Cómo se llaman?

_____   _____   _____

Nombre _____

Conexión con la salud

As you know, stress isn't just something that happens to adults. Children can suffer from it, too, if they work too hard or do too many activities. We all need to be aware of it and change some aspects of our lives in order to be healthier and feel more relaxed.

Imagine this is your weekly schedule. Make all necessary changes to turn your life into a less stressful one. Put together your new schedule below.

HORARIO ACTUAL	lunes	martes	miércoles	jueves	viernes
mañanas	• clase de natación • escuela	• gimnasio • escuela	• clase de piano • escuela	• clase de japonés • escuela	• clase de piano • escuela
tardes	• biblioteca	• clase de japonés	• fútbol	• biblioteca	• fútbol

NUEVO HORARIO	lunes	martes	miércoles	jueves	viernes
mañanas	dormir más horas				
tardes					

Now, explain the changes you made.

El lunes por la mañana no voy a ir a la clase de natación y voy a dormir

más horas.

_____

_____

⚜ ¡APRENDE MÁS! ⚜   **Nombre** _____

In Spanish, as in English, there are more ways than one to state the time. Often Spanish speaking people use the verb *faltar,* which means "to be lacking," to state the time before the hour. Occasionally, you will hear Spanish-speaking people who have lived in the United States adapt their language to the English form. Look at the clock below and read three ways you may hear people answer the question: *¿Qué hora es?*

1. Son las cinco menos veinticinco.
2. Faltan veinticinco minutos para las cinco.
3. Son las cuatro y treinta y cinco.

The first sentence follows the way you are learning. Spanish-speaking people all over the world will understand you if you use this pattern.

The second sentence uses the verb **faltar.** It is a way of saying "It's twenty-five to five."

The third sentence uses Spanish words with the English way of telling time. It's the same as saying, "It's four thirty-five."

Read the following examples, then write the same time in the way you have learned.

1. Faltan veinte minutos para las diez.

2. Son las nueve y cuarenta.

3. _____

1. Faltan quince minutos para la una.

2. Son las doce y cuarenta y cinco.

3. _____

Nombre _____

La página de diversiones

¿Quién tiene la pelota?

Detective Carlota Curiosa has been called to the Colegio Juárez to find out who took a soccer ball from the gymnasium. All she knows is that the ball *(la pelota)* was there on Tuesday at 1:00 P.M., but it was missing at 2:00 P.M. As a detective in training, you must read the testimony from the suspects and form your own conclusion!

Mario del Barrio

P: ¿A qué hora vas al gimnasio?

R: Siempre voy al gimnasio a las dos en punto. Tengo una clase a las dos.

Señor Olvida

P: ¿Cuándo va usted al gimnasio?

R: Voy al gimnasio a las dos menos veinte. Busco un globo. Mario practica deportes con mis globos.

Susana Banda

P: ¿Qué haces a la una de la tarde?

R: Siempre voy a la clase de música a la una en punto. Voy al gimnasio a las nueve de la mañana.

Señora Rústica

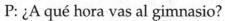

P: ¿Cuándo va usted al gimnasio?

R: A veces voy al gimnasio a la una menos cuarto. Me gusta practicar deportes. Los martes voy a la biblioteca.

¿Quién tiene la pelota?

_____ tiene la pelota.

Mira la página 114 para la solución.

¿Cómo se dice?

Nombre _____

A. What can you see in your classes? Match the pictures with the names of the classes. (Be careful: some classes relate to more than one picture.)

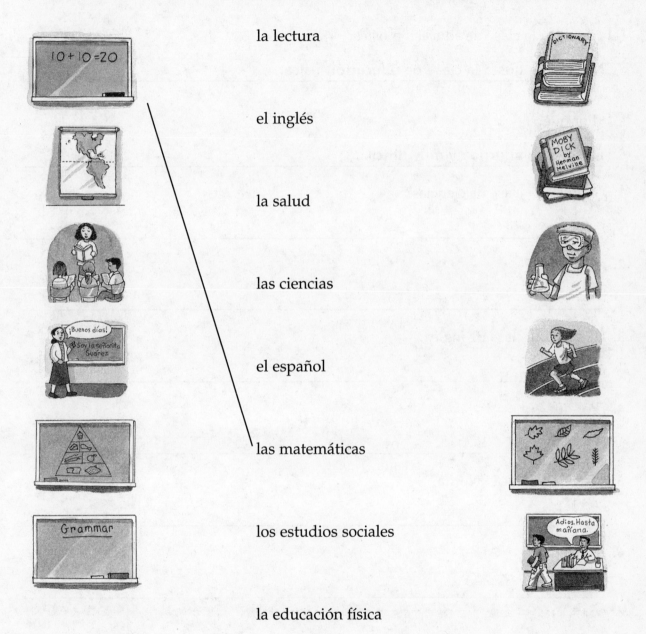

la lectura

el inglés

la salud

las ciencias

el español

las matemáticas

los estudios sociales

la educación física

¿Cómo se dice?

Nombre _____

A. Gabriela is interviewing you to find out which classes you like best. Write your answers.

M ¿Te gusta la clase de educación física?

No, no me gusta la clase de educación física. _____

M ¿Por qué?

La clase es aburrida y muy difícil. _____

1. ¿Te gusta la clase de ciencias?

_____

2. ¿Por qué?

_____

3. ¿Te gusta la clase de inglés?

_____

4. ¿Por qué?

_____

5. ¿Cuál es tu clase favorita?

_____

6. ¿Por qué?

_____

Solución a **¿Quién tiene la pelota?** de la página 112.

_____**El señor Olvida**_____ tiene la pelota.

¿Cómo se dice?

Nombre _____

A. You and Elvira are making T-shirts for your friends. Each shirt will have a picture of something each friend likes or dislikes. Answer Elvira's questions according to the faces.

M ¿A Carlos le gusta el arte?

 Sí, le gusta el arte. _____

_____

3. ¿A Norma le gustan las clases?

 _____

_____

1. ¿A Javier le gusta el invierno?

 _____

4. ¿A Paco le gustan los osos?

 _____

2. ¿A Inés le gustan los libros?

 _____

_____

5. ¿A Lola le gustan los niños?

 _____

_____

¡Piénsalo!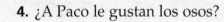

Answer the question below and then draw a design of what you like on the T-shirt.

¿Qué te gusta?

_____

_____

_____

Nombre _____

B. You and Elvira are ready to give your friends these T-shirts. Tell what each person likes or doesn't like. Use the picture and the name to write a sentence.

M

A Diego no le gustan los deportes.

_____

3.

_____

_____

1.

_____

_____

4.

_____

_____

2.

_____

_____

5.

_____

_____

¿Cómo se dice?

Nombre _____

A. You have written a message to your key pal in Venezuela. Use the appropriate form of the word in parentheses to complete each sentence.

11 de enero

¡Hola, Óscar!

¿Cómo estás? Estoy muy bien. (**M**) Yo _____escribo_____ (escribir) esta carta en la casa. (1) Yo _____ (aprender) el español en la escuela. (2) ¿_____ (aprender) tú el inglés? (3) ¿_____ (escribir) tú en inglés? (4) Yo _____ (leer) mucho en la clase de inglés. (5) Yo siempre _____ (comprender) las lecciones. (6) También _____ (pintar) mucho en la clase de arte. (7) Mi amigo Pepe también _____ (pintar). (8) En mi escuela, _____ (aprender) a usar las computadoras. (9) Y tú, ¿qué _____ (aprender)?

¡Hasta pronto!

_____
(tu nombre)

Nombre _____

B. You have been selected to appear with other "super-brains" on the game show *Los supercerebros*. Each contestant is given a situation and uses the clues to state what the subject does in that situation. Write the statements in your own words. Good luck!

M La maestra escribe una pregunta en el pizarrón. (El alumno / leer)

El alumno lee la pregunta.

1. Un compañero de clase tiene un número de teléfono. Tú tienes un cuaderno y un lápiz. (Yo / escribir)

   _____

2. Hace mucho frío. A Juanita le gusta practicar deportes. (Ella / patinar)

   _____

3. Enrique va a la biblioteca. Hay un libro interesante. (Él / leer)

   _____

4. La señora Molina lee libros en inglés. Ella escribe mucho en inglés. (Ella / comprender)

   _____

5. Tú lees la lección de estudios sociales. Escribes todas las respuestas. (Yo / comprender)

   _____

6. Diego va a la clase de computadoras. La clase es muy aburrida. Él nunca escribe en el cuaderno. Nunca tiene razón. (Él / no aprender)

   _____

¡A leer!

Nombre _____

Read the letter that Paula wrote to her key pal in Guatemala and fill out the chart below.

Las clases de Paula

Querido Javier:

Me gusta mucho la escuela. Tengo muchas clases este año. ¡La clase de español es fantástica! Aprendo mucho. La clase de lectura es difícil. Hay muchos libros y muchas tareas. Mi clase favorita es la clase de música. Allí voy a cantar y bailar con mis amigos. La clase de arte es divertida también. Pinto y dibujo obras de arte muy interesantes. A las doce tengo clase de educación física; es aburrida. Tengo hambre y sueño a esa hora. ¡No quiero practicar deportes a las doce del mediodía!

La clase de matemáticas es fácil. Me gustan mucho los números. La clase de salud es terrible, ¡y no comprendo nada! No tengo suerte con la clase de estudios sociales tampoco. ¡Pero la clase de ciencias y de inglés son sensacionales!

Hasta pronto,
Paula

¿Qué clases le gustan y no le gustan a Paula? Escribe las clases en la columna correcta.

Le gusta	No le gusta
la clase de español	

Nombre _____

Conexión con las matemáticas

In class, select a work of art to exhibit in the front of the classroom. Then each student in class chooses one of these expressions to say what they think of the work of art. Write a checkmark for each time each expression is used.

Choose one symbol to represent your classmates. On the chart, draw as many symbols for each expression as the number of classmates who say that expression. Make a pictograph.

¡Es divertido! _____

¡Es fantástico! _____

¡Es interesante! _____

¡Es importante! _____

¡Es aburrido! _____

	Personas
¡Es divertido!	
¡Es fantástico!	
¡Es interesante!	
¡Es importante!	
¡Es aburrido!	

Expresa tus ideas

Nombre _____

The Explorers' Club is holding a special meeting at school on Saturday. The members are supposed to plan their summer trip. No one seems to be paying attention! Use the words below to write at least five sentences about the picture.

leer	estudiar	interesante	importante
escribir	aprender	terrible	divertido
gustar	comprender	mucho	fantástico

_____

_____

_____

_____

_____

_____

_____

_____

 **¡A DIVERTIRSE!** Nombre _____

Busca la palabra

Read each sentence. Look in the puzzle for the word or words in heavy black letters. Each word may appear across or down in the puzzle. When you find a word, circle it. One is done for you.

1. ✓ **Escribo con** un **lápiz** en el **cuaderno**.
2. A mí **me gusta** la **clase** de **salud**.
3. ¿A ti te **gustan** las **ciencias**?
4. La **lectura** es **aburrida**.
5. ¡Qué **terrible**! Paco no **comprende** la **lección**.
6. Siempre **aprendo mucho** en las clases.
7. La **pregunta** es **muy fácil**.

```
M  J  C  U  A  D  E  R  N  O  L  Q  R  Ñ
U  X  I  P  R  E  G  U  N  T  A  U  T  C
Y  L  E  C  T  U  R  A  Í  A  U  É  Q  O
M  O  N  X  T  Y  C  L  A  S  E  Z  A  N
E  S  C  R  I  B  O  V  E  N  T  A  N  A
P  A  I  B  G  E  M  U  C  H  O  M  U  L
A  L  A  Ó  R  F  P  L  A  B  R  E  S  E
G  U  S  T  A  T  R  Ñ  P  C  I  C  Ó  C
A  D  I  R  N  T  E  R  R  I  B  L  E  C
L  Á  P  I  Z  E  N  T  E  N  Z  R  Q  I
A  B  U  R  R  I  D  A  N  Á  B  P  R  Ó
S  I  E  M  P  R  E  D  D  B  R  U  R  N
S  O  G  U  S  T  A  N  O  F  Á  C  I  L
```

¿Cómo se dice?

Nombre _____

A. You love fantasy stories. The book you're reading now is about the president of Andalandia and the members of his family. You have drawn his family tree. Use the picture to complete the sentence.

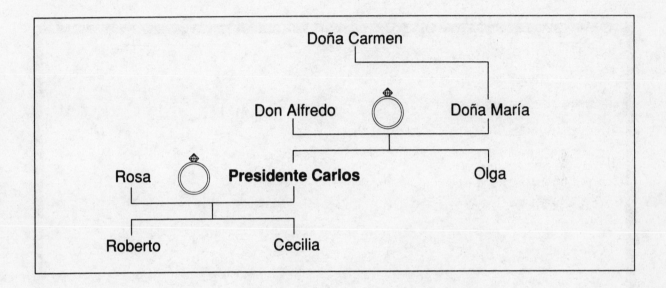

Doña Carmen

Don Alfredo   Doña María

Rosa   **Presidente Carlos**   Olga

Roberto   Cecilia

M Doña María es _____ la mamá _____ del presidente.

1. Olga es _____ del presidente.

2. Doña Carmen es _____ del presidente.

3. Roberto es _____ del presidente.

4. Don Alfredo es _____ del presidente.

5. Cecilia es _____ del presidente.

6. Don Alfredo y doña María son _____ del presidente.

¿Cómo se dice?

Nombre _____

A. What is your family tree like? Draw a family tree and write a paragraph about your family.

¿Cómo se dice?   Nombre _____

A. You have volunteered to work in the Lost and Found booth at the school carnival. What questions do you ask people? How do they answer you? Use *mi, mis, tu, tus, su,* or *sus* to complete each question and answer.

M  ¿Es __su__ perro?

Sí, es __mi__ perro.

M ¿Son __tus__ mapas?

Sí, son __mis__ mapas.

1.  ¿Es _____ hijo?

Sí, es _____ hijo.

4.  ¿Son _____ libros?

Sí, son _____ libros.

2.  ¿Es _____ papá?

Sí, es _____ papá.

5.  ¿Son _____ hijos?

Sí, son _____ hijos.

3.  ¿Son _____ loros?

Sí, son _____ loros.

6.  ¿Es _____ reloj?

Sí, es _____ reloj.

Nombre _____

B. Natán's relatives visited him on his birthday. He drew a picture of the grand family event and wrote a paragraph. Help him finish it.

(**M**) ___Mi___ familia es grande. (1) _____ abuelo se llama Adán. (2) _____ abuela se llama Irene. (3) _____ hermanos son León y Andrés. (4) Darío y Lucía son _____ tíos. (5) _____ hijos son Rubén y Hugo. (6) _____ hijas son Nora y Ema.

¿Cómo se dice?

Nombre _____

A. Look at the following people and write sentences to describe them. Use adjectives from the box below. You can use more than one for each, and you can use each adjective more than once. (Be careful: you will need to change the form of some adjectives).

alto	guapo	antipático	bajo	simpático	joven

Señora Luna   Señor García   Alejandra   Señora Flores   Señor Flores   Hugo   Señora Márquez   Señor Moreno

M   Señora Luna es antipática. _____

M   Señor García es bajo. _____

_____

_____

_____

_____

_____

Nombre _____

B. Have you met Valentina's family? Look at the portrait and complete the sentences.

M _____ **Andrea, su madre,** _____ es simpática.

1. _____ es alta.

2. _____ es bajo.

3. _____ es guapo.

4. _____ son viejos.

5. _____ son antipáticos.

6. _____ son jóvenes.

7. _____ es baja.

C. What is your family like? Write five sentences about your family members. On a separate sheet of paper, make a portrait that reflects what you wrote.

_____

_____

_____

_____

¡A leer!

Nombre _____

Read about Óscar's family. Then answer the questions.

La familia de Óscar

Me llamo Oscar Guzmán Pérez y me gusta mucho jugar al fútbol. Tengo diez años. Vivo en Costa Rica con mis papás, mi abuelita Berta y mi hermanito Rubén. Rubén es un bebé. ¡Ah!, y nuestro gato es Pufito.

Me gusta jugar con Rubén, pero tiene sólo dieciocho meses y todavía no habla bien. A quien más quiero es a la abuelita Berta, la mamá de mi papá. Por las noches, cuando voy a dormir, siempre me cuenta historias divertidas.

> Nota:
> **Me cuenta** means *tells me.*

1. ¿Cuántos años tiene Óscar? ¿Dónde vive?

_____

2. ¿Cuántos hermanos tiene Óscar? ¿Cómo se llaman?

_____

3. ¿Qué animal tiene la familia de Óscar? ¿Cómo se llama?

_____

4. ¿Por qué el hermanito no habla bien?

_____

5. ¿Quién es la mamá del papá de Óscar?

_____

6. ¿Qué hace siempre la abuelita Berta por las noches?

_____

Nombre _____

Conexión con la cultura

Do you remember that people in many Spanish-speaking countries use both parents' last names *(los apellidos)*? Traditionally, the father's last name goes first, and the mother's maiden name goes second.

Get together with four classmates. Write what your full name would be based on this custom. Ask your classmates for their father's last name and for their mother's maiden name and write it down.

Nombre	Primer apellido	Segundo apellido

 ¡APRENDE MÁS!

Nombre _____

A suffix is a set of letters that you attach to the end of a word to give the word a different meaning. For example, the endings **-ito, -itos, -ita,** and **-itas** are suffixes. When you add them to the end of a word, you change the meaning to indicate smallness or affection.

Compare the following lists of words in Spanish and English:

Spanish		English	
rojo	roj**izo**	red	redd**ish**
el niño	la niñ**ez**	child	child**hood**
tonto	la tonte**ría**	foolish	foolish**ness**
blanco	la blanc**ura**	white	white**ness**
el amigo	la amis**tad**	friend	friend**ship**
terrible	terrible**mente**	terrible	terrib**ly**

In each example, the meaning of the word changes because the suffix was added. When you know how suffixes work, you have a good clue to guessing the meanings of new words.

See how well you can spot a suffix. Read the following sentences and underline each word that you think has a suffix.

Me gusta la frescura de la mañana.   I like the coolness of the morning.

Diana aprende fácilmente.   Diana learns easily.

No me gusta la oscuridad de la noche.   I don't like the darkness of the night.

La verdura del verano es bella.   The greenness of summer is pretty.

☺ ¡A DIVERTIRSE! ☺   **Nombre** _____

La sopa de letras

**Find the secret words in the alphabet soup. Cross out the letters for each
word in the list. With the letters that are left, form the secret words.**

papá	hermano	hijo	mamá	nieto
nieta	abuela	hermana	hija	abuelo

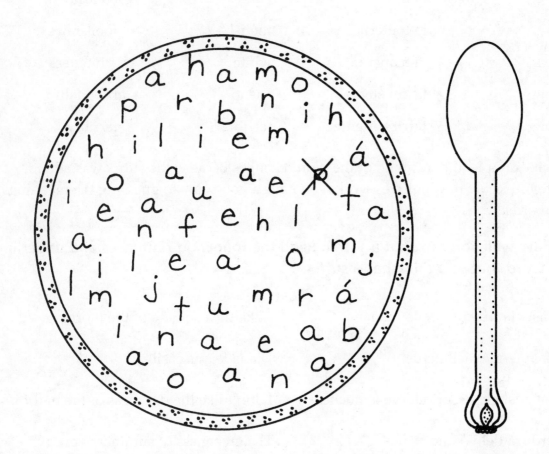

Las palabras secretas: _____ _____   __ __ __ __ __ __

Nombre _____

A. Write a sentence using *tener* that describes what is happening
to the boy in the picture.

Tiene frío. _____

5. _____

1.  _____

6.  _____

2.  _____

7.  _____

3.  _____

8.  _____

4.  _____

9. _____

Nombre _____

B. Look at this mixed-up conversation. In one of them, Pedro, an 8-year-old boy, is talking to his music teacher. In the other, Emma and Juana are talking. Can you put the conversations together?

_____ Muy bien, gracias. ¿Y tú?

_____ No, yo voy a clase de inglés.

_____ Bien, gracias. ¿Va a la clase de música?

_____ Yo voy a clase de inglés.

_____ Bien, gracias. ¿Te gusta la clase de música?

_____ Hola, ¿cómo estás?

__✓__ Buenos días, Srta. Álvarez. ¿Cómo está usted?

_____ Muy bien, ¿y tú, Emma?

_____ Sí, ¿y tú, a qué clase vas?

_____ Sí, mucho. Ahora voy a clase de música. ¿Y tú?

Pedro y su maestra: **Emma y Juana:**

Buenos días, Srta. Álvarez. ¿Cómo está usted?   _____

_____   _____

_____   _____

_____   _____

Nombre _____

C. Here's a short interview about your weekly activities. Answer each question, saying on which day and at what time (or in which part of the day) you do these things:

M ¿Cuándo vas a la biblioteca?

Voy a la biblioteca los lunes y los jueves por la tarde.

1. ¿Cuándo estudias?

_____

2. ¿Cuándo caminas por el parque?

_____

3. ¿Cuándo usas la computadora?

_____

4. ¿Cuándo practicas deportes?

_____

5. ¿Cuándo vas al cine?

_____

6. ¿Cuándo vas a clase de arte?

_____

7. ¿Cuándo vas a la escuela?

_____

8. ¿Cuándo vas a comprar a la tienda?

_____

9. ¿Cuándo vas a jugar a la casa de tus amigos?

_____

Nombre _____

D. What class are these people talking about? Read the answers and write the questions, using the verb *gustar*.

M ¿Te gustan las ciencias? _____

—Sí, mucho. Me gusta la naturaleza, los animales...

1. _____

—¿Las matemáticas? Sí, mucho.

2. _____

—¿A Elsa? Sí, mucho. Ella tiene un globo y estudia las capitales.

3. _____

—Sí, porque me gusta leer historias como *The Jungle Book* o *Tom Sawyer*...

4. _____

—No. No me gustan los deportes.

5. _____

—No, porque no le gusta estudiar otras lenguas.

Nombre _____

E. You have taken these photos for the school yearbook.
Write captions for them. Use the verbs in the box.

| cocinar | leer | nadar | usar | comer |

M    **Ellos cocinan.** _____

1.   _____

2.    _____

3.    _____

4.    _____

Nombre _____

F. You are about to meet Carla's family. She has explained who everyone is, but it is really complicated! Now she has drawn her family tree to help you. Look at the tree and answer the questions.

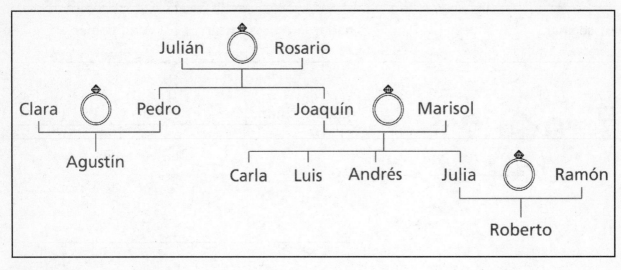

M ¿Quién es su abuelo?

Julián es su abuelo. _____

1. ¿Cómo se llaman sus tíos?

   _____

2. ¿Cuántos hermanos y hermanas tiene?

   _____

3. ¿Sus hermanos tienen hijos?

   _____

4. ¿Quién es Agustín?

   _____

5. ¿Quién es la abuela de Carla?

   _____

6. ¿Cómo se llama el sobrino de Carla?

   _____